Repair Order, Documentation Basics

Charles P. Hillier

DEDICATION

To all the Technicians that work to keep the economy
on the move in all types of weather and time of day.

CONTENTS

PREFACE

The reason for this book is quite simple. I was on vacation and was stuck inside due to severe storms. Having nothing to do I turned on the T.V., not knowing the only thing on was the Peoples Court Marathon. I was sitting there and watching - and it just so happened that the first case was for a repair facility that was in litigation for improper repairs. After the Judge interviewed the plaintiff and asked for the invoice, she reviewed it. She then started questioning the repair shop owner. The judge asked what was done and after the shop owner stated the repairs, she tore into him due to the repair order being poorly written and vague. The shop lost the suit and damaged its reputation. This was just one of the numerous suits adjudicated that day. I was amazed at the number of service providers that were lost due to insufficient documentation. I asked myself how anyone who charges for services rendered could be so lax as to not properly document and invoice charges correctly.

ACKNOWLEDGMENTS

To my loving wife and children with whose support all things are possible

1 AN EXPENSIVE LESSON

If you have been in the service industry for any length of time, you have dealt with customers that have been upset with the services provided. Regardless of justified or not, you now have a disgruntled customer. Now the issue is what will they do?

Most often, they do nothing but express their anger and leave to never be seen again. However, occasionally you have a customer who will not calm down. The next thing you know you have the police at your door because either you called them or the customer did. The police show up and everyone calms down and they leave, or so you thought.

The following weeks go by and you forget all about it, then one day you get a summons to small claims court. You look at the summons and recognize the name; you think there is no way you will lose. You performed the repair as requested, you charged accordingly and the vehicle drove out, with no problem.

You gather the documents you think you will need and call your attorney. He agrees to meet you for lunch and you tell him what happened. Your attorney looks over your paperwork and thinks you are good to go but offers to come along if you want. You say no, that you should be able to handle it.

The big day comes you dress nice and bring the technician along with you. After standing around for 2 hours you are called. The judge starts by questioning the plaintiff. They start by stating the dents and scratches were not there when they dropped off the vehicle. However, were there when they picked up the vehicle and the rattle they brought it in for was still there. To make it worse it broke down the next day.

The customer now sobbing hands their copy of the invoice for $1,442.00 to the judge. Now it is your turn. The first question the judge asks you is if the damages are documented. You look at the repair order and find nothing noted, and your heart sinks. You tell the judge no they are not. Next, the judge asks what repairs was the vehicle brought in for. You state a rattle under the vehicle.

The judge asks how did you fix it? You state the catalyst broke loose inside the catalytic converter and you told them that they needed to replace the catalytic converter. You also recommended the muffler due to it might still rattle if not replaced due to pieces from the converter that could now be in the muffler. The judge asked if they approved replacing both items.

You reply they approved the converter but declined the muffler. You state when they declined the muffler; they were told that it might still rattle when they came to get the vehicle. The judge then asked the plaintiff if that is true. They said no they were never told that. The judge asks where was that noted that they declined the muffler. Again you look at the repair order, now you feel sick. You reply it was not. Now the judge is upset and asks you if is this the normal way you do business. You are at a loss for words. As you, give your paperwork to the judge.

The judge asks the plaintiff if there is a tow bill for the breakdown and of course, there is one for $250.00, and hands an invoice for the tow and a bill to put a new exhaust for $556.00, along with a body shop estimate for $985.00 to fix the dents. The judge comes back and says judgment for the plaintiff for $3233.00. You are shocked and upset you lost. To make matters worse you not only give them back their money but you even paid to replace the muffler and fix the dents on their vehicle.

2 RULES AND REGULATIONS

It is an accepted standard regardless of what type of services are being billed, that written documentation must provide support for charges being invoiced/billed.

Most industries have some form of regulation, whether administered by a professional organization, State Board, or governmental statute. They all specify the information required to make the invoice comply with their requirements. Often these rules and regulations go unknown until issues arise with the invoice in question.

Very few shops know what is exactly required. This often results in these documents lacking critical information that is required by law. By missing required information, you open the door for the State to levy and collect fines, lawsuits from the customer, or chargebacks from the manufacturer during an audit. Regardless of the reason, the outcome is the same, a loss of income.

The following guidelines are intended to help repair facilities understand issues relating to billing and documentation. For billing purposes, repair facilities are to follow billing and documentation guidelines requirements established by regulating authorities.

Repair facilities must be up to date with their local and state requirements, all the while being attentive to the quality of their written documentation. Successful facilities all recognize that proper documentation not only improves repairs but also improves the ability to collect for services and reduces the repair facility's legal exposure.
As a repair facility, the repair order/invoice is a legal document that is universally accepted for repairs in most disputes.

The repair order should only include repairs that are

"Reasonable and Necessary" for the diagnosis and/or repair of a malfunctioning system/part

Reasonable and Necessary Services

Services and items considered "Reasonable and Necessary" must be established as:

- Safe and effective.
- Consistent with the symptoms and/or diagnosis of the concern under investigation.
- Consistent with accepted professional standards and repair procedures.
- Provided at the most appropriate level of repair or concern.

Unreasonable and Unnecessary services

Services and items considered "Unreasonable and Unnecessary" include those that are:

- Not generally accepted in the Service community as safe and effective in the setting and for the condition for which it is used.
- Not proven to be safe and effective based on authoritative evidence ;(not following published repair procedures).
- Experimental; (unapproved test/replacement procedures that may result in a component or progressive damages).
- Not supported in the repair procedure.
- Furnished at a level, duration, or frequency that is not appropriate; (excessive duplication of test/repair procedures that yield no useful information).
- Not furnished under accepted standards of repair practice.
- Not furnished in a setting appropriate to the conditions.
- Improperly performed.

3 THE START

It all starts when the customer shows up at your facility for repairs.

The arrival of the Customer in your service center is the first step of the repair process. Up to that point, all you may have is a name on a planner along with a basic description of the concern. Once the customer is at your location, the Service Advisor needs to greet them courteously and professionally and be empathetic to their needs.

The Advisor must begin the repair process by making all required entries on the write-up form while completing the inspection, noting any damages and safety issues.

Once the inspection is completed then the interview can begin. The customer interview is a crucial step in the repair process. During this time, the advisor listens to their description of the Concerns or service requested. These are to be noted as the customers' concerns.

Once the interview is completed, then the advisor reads back the concerns to the customer to validate that the concerns are correct and there is no other work being requested. Once this is confirmed the adviser then has the customer sign the release agreeing to the terms of repairs.

The next step is to enter the concerns from the write-up sheet into the repair order system.
• Write a clear and complete explanation of the owner's concerns and instructions to the technician.
• This should be a detailed, to-the-point description of how the customer described his/her concern. Use basic abbreviations.
• Assign a separate line for each customer concern.

The repair order is logged into the Management System and then assigned to the technician. The technician needs to review the repair order paying special attention to the concerns, and then question him or herself- "Is there enough information to accurately begin diagnosis of the vehicle?" If not the technician needs to review with the advisor to gain more information.

Example:

☐ The customer states "vehicle has a strange noise that comes on the dash area after the vehicle has run for a while"

In this write-up, the concern may not have been duplicated and the vehicle returned to the customer as no problem was found, or a repair was performed for what the technician took as the concern but was incorrect. Either way, the outcome is not acceptable to the customer, and will be sure to return upset.

If a good description is found, the technician then proceeds to the next step of the repair process. The technician clocks on to repair and begins with the duplication of concern. This is where a good description of concern is critical.

Example:

☐ The customer states "vehicle has a strange noise from the passenger's side when the a/c, has been on for a while."

In this write-up, the technician was able to duplicate the concern. The technician then did a vehicle bulletin search. That resulted in a document for a noisy A/C issue that stated the expansion valve is prone to a vibration that the customer may present as a concern of a whooping noise in the passenger side of the dash.

Charles Hillier

SUBJECT: A/C EXPANSION VALVE NOISE			No: **TSB-03-55-010**
			DATE: **October, 2003**
			MODEL: **2C**
CIRCULATE TO:	[ ] GENERAL MANAGER	[X] PARTS MANAGER	[X] TECHNICIAN
[X] SERVICE ADVISOR	[X] SERVICE MANAGER	[ ] WARRANTY PROCESSOR	[ ] SALES MANAGER

PURPOSE

Customers may complain of a "whooping" noise coming from the passenger side of the instrument panel, which occurs in high ambient temperatures and high humidity conditions during normal A/C operation. If the noise is heard during PDI, or if a customer complains of this noise, install the new, improved A/C expansion valve listed in the "PARTS INFORMATION" section of this bulletin.

4 CONCERNS ARE DUPLICATED

Once the concern is duplicated and the repair begins, at this point, the technician needs to be conscious of the repairs he is performing, and the steps included.

PROCEDURE

Replace the A/C expansion valve as follows:

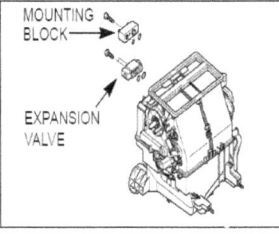

1. Discharge the A/C system.

2. From the engine side, remove the A/C hoses from the mounting block.

3. Loosen the mounting block screws.

4. Remove the expansion valve screws.

5. Use the mounting block bolt to remove the expansion valve.

6. Install the new, improved expansion valve listed in the PARTS INFORMATION section of this bulletin.

7. Inspect the A/C hoses and O-rings. Replace if any damage is found.

8. Reinstall the mounting block and A/C hoses.

9. Recharge the A/C system with 560-600 g (19.75-21.16 oz) refrigerant.

This is where errors and inconsistencies in time reporting continue to be a problem. Facilities are often lax in the enforcement of proper repair time documentation. All too often technicians lose track of when to log in and off each repair. Technicians often just continue with a diagnosis until the cause is determined, then log off. This may have caused an issue if multiple systems or tests were performed. Most manufacturers require a separate timestamp for each labor operation performed.

Time documentation is one of the most overlooked steps in the repair process. The importance of this step cannot be overstated; failure to correctly document diagnosis and repair times will result in incorrect tracking of the technician's time resulting in challenges to the amount of labor charged to the final invoice as well as result in the actual cost of the repairs being misreported. Failure to properly document the time required to perform repairs may also result in a chargeback during manufacture audits.

Repair time is defined as the period during which Technician is present and working on customers' concerns. It starts when the technician begins the repair services in the service bay or an equivalent area and ends when the technician is no longer furnishing services to the vehicle/component, or When the repair is safely completed.

Discription
Test drive vehicle, found noise in passenger side of dash Performed bulletin search found TSB 03-55-010 expansion valve. Performed TSB retested vehicle noise gone.
Time Recorded
Time on 7:02 08/23/2014   tech 125
Time off 11:00 08/23/2014   tech 125
Total time 3.98

Based on the definition the labor time documented above should be invoiced for 3.98 hours. The issue upon review of the time documentation is the tech failed to punch off when returned from the test drive, no documentation of how long was spent doing research or obtaining parts. They also failed to properly document the actual repair time for the repair.

Then failed again to document labor to support that he verified repairs. It also indicates the technician took no breaks during the repair. This would raise many flags about the validity and accuracy of the time documentation for this repair. If audited by the manufacturer would be challenged.

The correct time documentation would reflect each step of the repair. Test drive, begin the repair, break, finish repair and the test drive to verify the repair.

Discription		
Test drive vehicle, found noise in passenger side of dash Performed bulletin search found TSB 03-55-010 expansion valve. Performed TSB retested vehicle noise gone.		
Time Recorded		
Time on 7:02 08/23/2014	tech 125	
Time off 7:17 08/23/2014	tech 125	
Time on 7:42 08/23/2014	tech 125	
Time off 8:57 08/23/2014	tech 125	
Time on 9:14 08/23/2014	tech 125	
Time off 9:41 08/23/2014	tech 125	
Time on 9:44 08/23/2014	tech 125	
Time off 9:59 08/23/2014	tech 125	
Total time 1.72		

This time documentation is within the labor established for the repair if you figure out the test drive times.

WARRANTY INFORMATION

A/C Expansion Valve

Nature Code: 806　　　　　　　*Cause Code:* 990

Labor Operation No. 55151210　　*Time Allowance:* 1.2 hrs.

The next step is to have the technician document the cause and correction. This includes documentation of what diagnosis was performed and what was determined to be the root cause of the concern.

Cause: This must include why the repair is necessary / identification of the defect as determined by the Technician.--- *Explain damage* (e.g., *Expansion valve noisy.*)

Correction: Describe repair steps performed to resolve the cause (e.g., *Replace expansion valve per TSB # 03-55-010*)

5 DIAGNOSTIC STEPS

These notes must include all diagnostic steps and any documents used during the repair. This is often an overlooked part of the repair documentation. This often results in lost revenues due to incomplete or partial stories. All technician notes should use the S.O.A. P. S. method for documenting repairs

The S stands for SUBJECT (something that is being discussed, examined, or otherwise dealt with), and the subject is the vehicle the technician should inspect the vehicle and take note of its condition. Is the vehicle in good working order that shows no obvious signs of neglect or abuse?

The O for Objective (based on facts rather than thoughts or opinions),

The technician should be taking an objective look at the repair history and any bulletins that have been released for the make and model they are about to repair.

The A for Assessment (judgment about something based on an understanding of the situation), what are the symptoms or systems involved and what tests were required to diagnose those systems, what tools were required. Documentation must be comprehensive and complete to support repairs. Increasingly, written documentation is also used for, research, quality assurance, and legal review

The P for Plan (something that somebody intends or has arranged to do) at this point in the repair process the technician wound have determined the root cause, inspected the related systems for progressive damages, and developed a repair plan to resolve the concern.

The S for Summation (a summary of something that has been said or written) should be a high-level summary of the Concern cause and correction for the service writer so the repair order can be closed out and the appropriate parties invoiced for the repairs

The example below is a poorly written repair order note missing the required information: no repair order#, no tech #, no customer signature, no parts listed, and no date of repair. Depending on the state, this could result in severe fines.

Concern

The example below is for a customer repair order that is complete take note that all fields are filled out with the required information including in and out mileage, in and out time, dates and authorization notes, and recommended services.

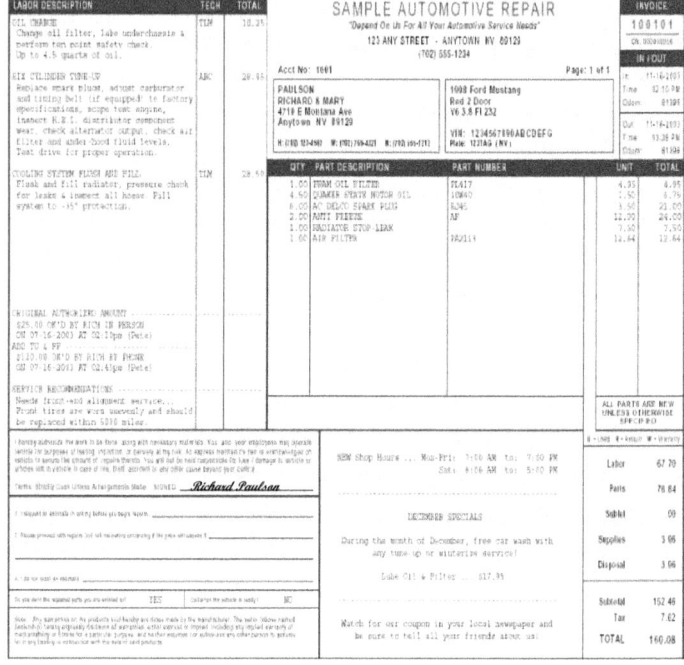

If a vehicle requires additional repairs not requested at the initial write-up or not covered in the original order, an estimate for the added cost must be prepared and the customer contacted for permission to do the work. When the customer authorizes additional work, the advisor must document the additional authorization. If the authorization was verbal or by telephone, you must make the same notations on the final invoice as that of the work order.

If an additional authorization was by fax, you must attach a copy of the fax document that is signed and dated by the customer that shows the date, time of transmission, and a description of the additional repairs, parts, labor, and additional cost.

If an additional authorization was by e-mail, you must attach a copy of the E-mail authorization, which shows the date, time of transmission, and a description of the additional repairs, parts, labor, and additional cost.

Charles Hillier

ABOUT THE AUTHOR

Educated at Elgin Community College. His career
encompasses all aspects of repair facilities operations. He
is also a Certified Instructor for the state of Illinois (5 years
as an instructor) Worked with AYES and NATEF in the
certification of High schools. He obtained Master
Certified Technician status from numerous manufacturers.
His Current duties include managing the U.S. Dealer labor
rates along with Regional Warranty Training and
administration for vehicle manufacture.

This book is intended to provide information on repair
order documentation, with the understanding that the
publisher and author are not engaged in rendering legal,
accounting, or other professional services. If legal or other
expert assistance is required, the services of a competent
professional   should   be   sought.